P9-DFS-285

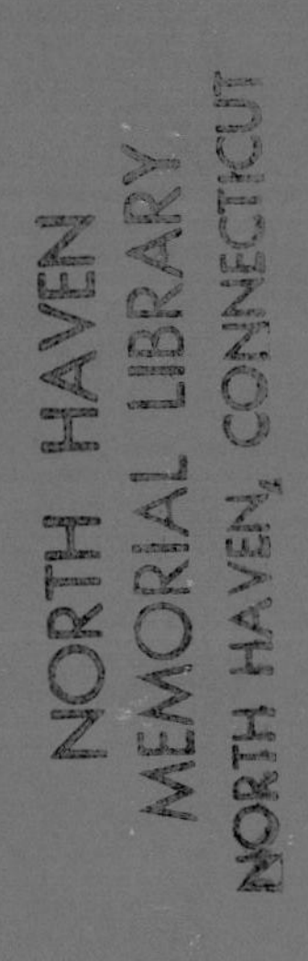
NORTH HAVEN
MEMORIAL LIBRARY
NORTH HAVEN, CONNECTICUT

# A WEEKEND WITH PICASSO

# A WEEKEND WITH PICASSO

by Florian Rodari

RIZZOLI
NEW YORK

First published in the United States of America in 1991 by
Rizzoli International Publications, Inc.
300 Park Avenue South, New York, New York 10010



Library of Congress Cataloging-in-Publication Data
Rodari, Florian
[Dimanche avec Picasso. English]
A weekend with Picasso / by Florian Rodari.
p. cm.
Translation of: Un dimanche avec Picasso.
Summary: The twentieth-century artist talks about his life and work as if entertaining the reader for a weekend.
ISBN 0-8478-1437-8
1. Picasso, Pablo, 1881–1973–Juvenile literature. 2. Artists–France–Biography–Juvenile literature. [1. Picasso, Pablo. 1881–1973. 2. Artists.] I. Title II. Title: Picasso.
N6853.P3R5713 1991
709'.2–dc20
91-12427
CIP
AC

Design by Mary McBride

Printed in Great Britain

It's the weekend—time to rest—but, as you can see, I'm working. We artists never take time off, we're always thinking about what we're going to do next! Even when we seem to be resting, our brains are going a mile a minute, and very often, late at night, when everyone else in the house is asleep, we go back to the studio . . . I can't help myself—when my hands want to create something there's just no stopping them. They grab whatever's within reach—paper, modeling clay, old rags, bits of wood or cardboard—and they shape, fold, paint, carve, cut, nail, or glue them together . . . or they sign my name, which you may very well know . . .

My hands, sometimes they're like mischievous little puppets, dancing in front of me, inventing new stories, playing tricks, building castles that they tear down and build up again. Amused, my eyes follow them, but if I try to scold them or to make them stop their antics, I find it's impossible—they're already somewhere else, doing something almost without my permission, making other figures, sketching new portraits. And so, for me, work is something like play, and when you play, as you know, you forget about time.

I feel as if I'm still a child like you, and when they call me from downstairs for the umpteenth time, shouting: "Pablo Picasso, come down this minute—dinner's on the table. . . . Picasso, please come, the guests are here," I pay no attention and just go on working with my pencils and brushes. When I am excited about something I'm working on, I couldn't care less about eating, sleeping, or seeing people, I just want to finish what I have started.

*Before turning this page, look again at the previous page: when he was over ninety years old, Picasso still drew himself as* The Young Artist—*you could say that he felt his work kept him from growing old!*

Don't worry about the mess you see in the living room. I use this room as my studio, and all of my studios (I've had many, in Barcelona, Spain, where I grew up; in Paris and also in the south of France) have soon been crammed full of all kinds of strange objects. But watch out! If anyone tried to touch anything, I'd be furious. Why? Let me explain: we artists are a bit like ragpickers, we like to have all sorts of odds and ends around us. They may seem completely useless to other people—but you never know! These things can lie around for years sometimes, in a corner, behind a pile of books or a stack of paintings. They may get all covered with dust and seem to be completely forgotten. Then one day we happen to glance at them and lo! the magic that first attracted us is there again, and so we bring them back to life in a painting or sculpture.

Any object, even the most unlikely, something broken-down or seemingly useless, can give us ideas: a stovepipe, a broken jug, a breadbasket, a pebble found at the beach, the skull of a goat, a toy, a gardening tool . . . Sometimes it's the shape that appeals to us, it suddenly looks like a face or a kind of animal. At other times it's the color or the material that reminds us of something else. For painters, every object has a secret, mysterious life of its own.

*A curious eight-year old makes her way through the disorder of the studio that Picasso set up in the living room of the villa called La Californie, which he bought in 1955, near Cannes, in the south of France.*

But I discovered long ago that you can do more with these objects than simply draw them. Sometimes, of course, I do put them directly into my paintings, just as they are. And sometimes I make a sculpture by putting things together in new ways. For example, do you know those little toy cars that everyone has played with? Someone left one in my garden not so long ago. Well, I picked it up and after taking a good look at it and turning it every which way, I suddenly realized what it reminded me of—the long hood, the curved windshield, and the two headlights—it looked just like half of a monkey's head! So I brought it back to my studio, took off the wheels and springs, then ran to find another car that was almost exactly like it. Then I glued the two together, added a pair of coffee-cup handles for the ears, two marbles for the eyes, and look!—it's the head of this mother monkey! This kind of sculpture, made up of many different things assembled or gathered together, is called an "assemblage."

Oh, I've made lots of assemblages in just that way. The best known is one that I put together in the wink of an eye; by simply turning these handlebars around and attaching them to a bicycle seat, I transformed them into a bull's horns and head. The image of the bull's head was there, waiting for me to discover it inside the parts of the bicycle.

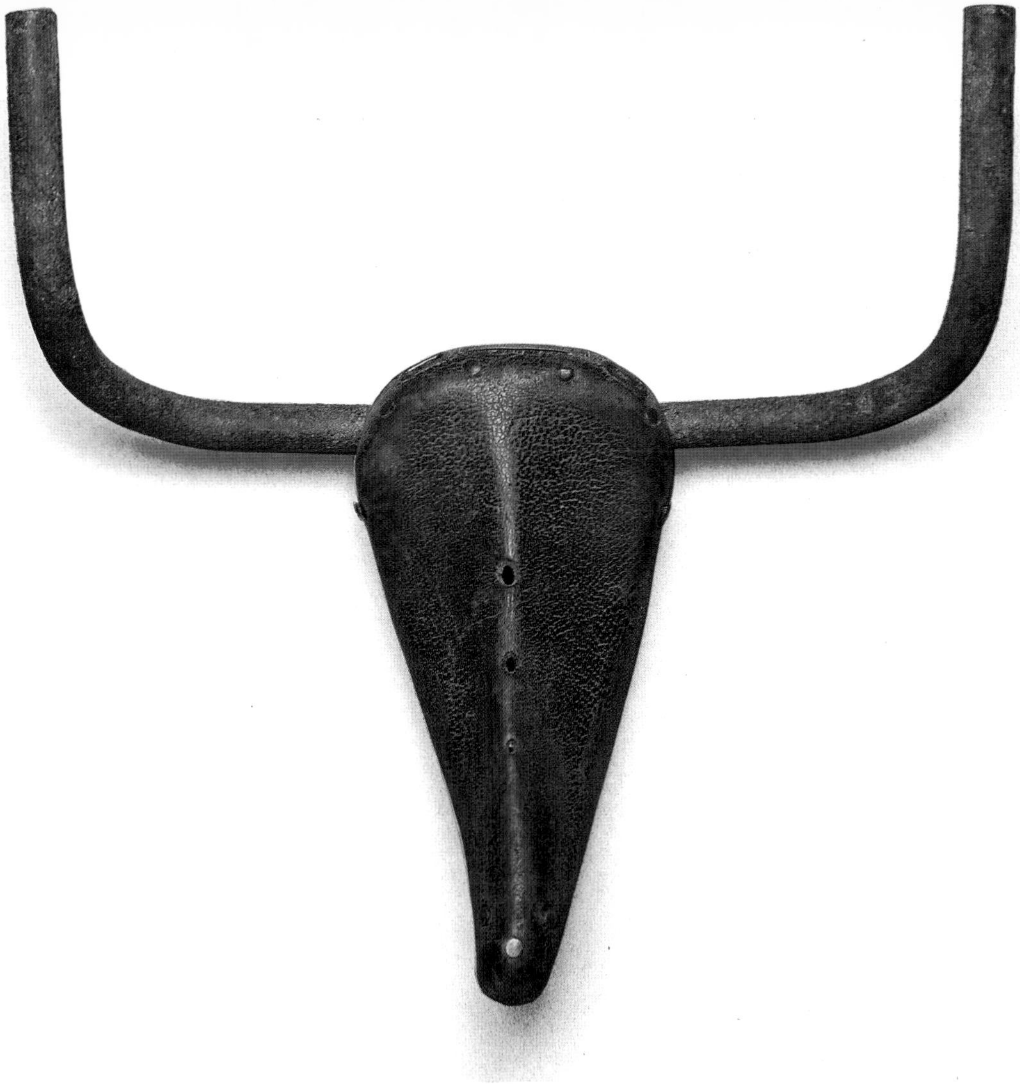

You see, you can use whatever's at hand; with just a few pieces of wood, a broomstick, the legs of a bed, you can make a figure like the one there, at the right. Look at it—isn't it funnier and more touching with its slightly ungainly simplicity, than if I'd tried to draw its parts in an exact way when I found them on the beach the other day?

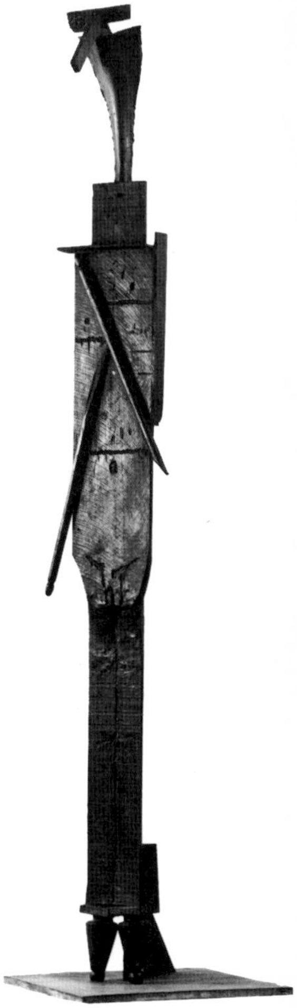

I almost always like to work quickly, to express only the essence of my subject, to make a detail suggest the whole. One day I wanted to do an etching of a bull. The first drawing I made looked almost like a real bull you might see in a field, with its tiny eyes, huge head, tufted tail, and four cloven hooves. A week later, I did another drawing. This time I left out a lot of detail in order to emphasize the animal's strength. Some time later, I took out all the shadows and reduced the beast almost to its bare bones. And finally, on the last try, in only a few strokes, I sketched just the "idea" of a bull. It is very simple, but it seems to me to be even more effective than the first picture I drew.

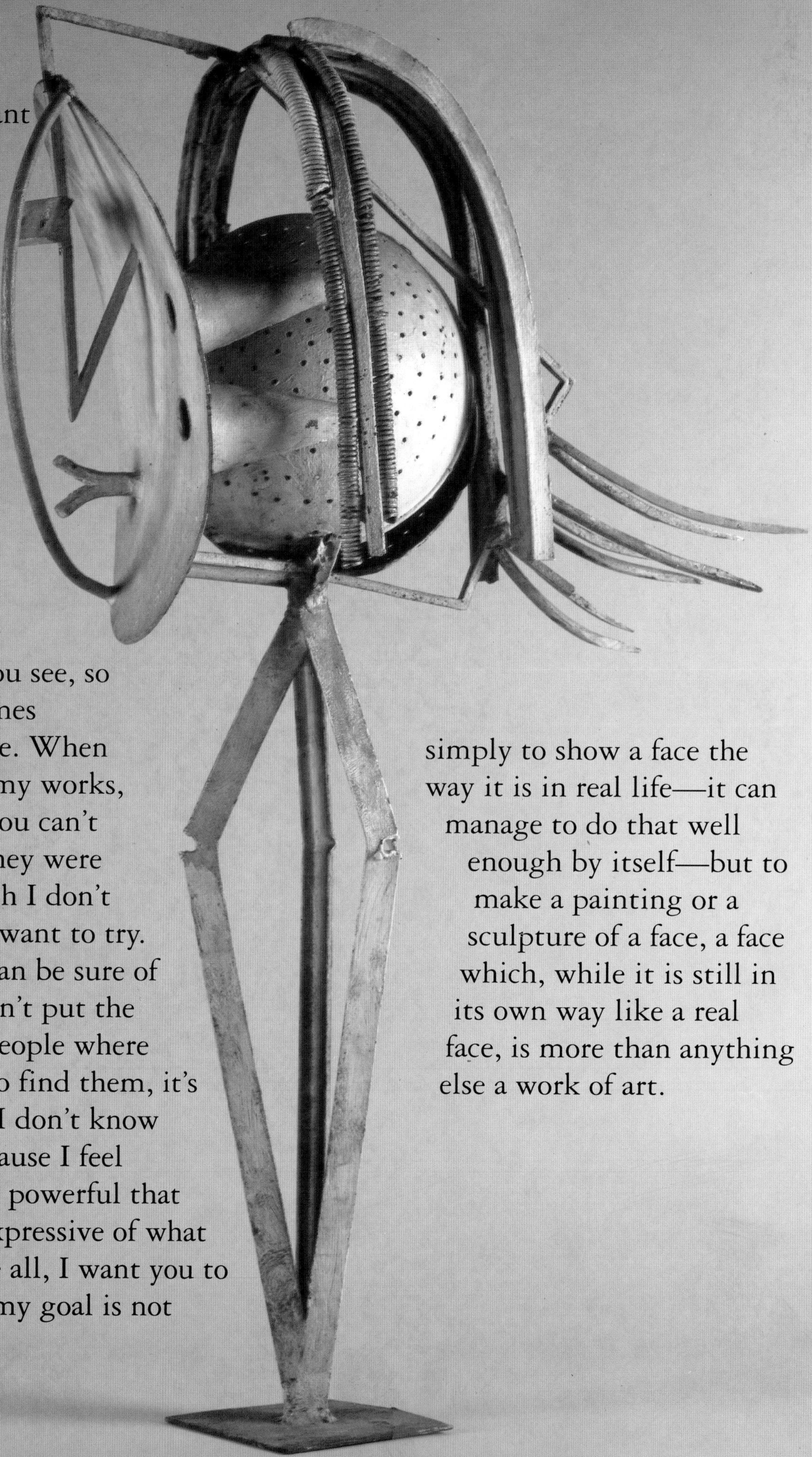

The important thing for me is not to have you recognize such and such a person's face or this or that animal. I'd like you to be surprised—and perhaps amused—by the image you see, so that it becomes unforgettable. When you look at my works, sometimes you can't guess how they were made, though I don't mind if you want to try.

But you can be sure of this—if I don't put the eyes of my people where you expect to find them, it's not because I don't know how but because I feel they're more powerful that way, more expressive of what I feel. Above all, I want you to understand my goal is not simply to show a face the way it is in real life—it can manage to do that well enough by itself—but to make a painting or a sculpture of a face, a face which, while it is still in its own way like a real face, is more than anything else a work of art.

Here are two ways of representing a woman's head: above, in a painting, and, on the left, by assembling pieces of objects from the junkyard—an old colander for the skull, some springs for the hair, and pieces of metal for the face.

I wouldn't be surprised if your drawing teacher, when he or she looked at the doodles in your notebooks, exclaimed: "Now there! Your grandfather would be proud of a grandchild like you! These scribbles are just like Picasso's!" Well, the dear teacher would be wrong, because at your age, I drew like the great Raphael who, for a long time, was looked up to by all painters. This means that I was able to draw all the differences in shading and lighting, to reproduce very carefully just what was in front of my eyes. When he saw how advanced I was at thirteen years old, my father, even though he was an excellent drawing teacher, said: "Here are my brushes and paints, Pablo, they are yours now." And he never painted again in his life. Well, perhaps that is a slight exaggeration, but he did recognize my talent.

By the time I was twenty years old, I could paint just about anything and began to have a lot of success showing my work. But very soon I realized that there was no point in just trying to copy nature, in trying to make things seem lifelike. A photograph could do that very well. But a painting should go beyond this.

It was obvious to me that when I painted a jug, I would never be able to drink any water from it, nor to pluck the strings of a guitar in a drawing. So I felt free to distort objects in my paintings, to stretch them out, flatten them harshly against the surface and fill in their outlines and forms with the most strident colors imaginable. People who were used to more conservative, realistic painting considered my work very daring, yet I was by no means the only artist to work in this way at the time. But, perhaps more than any of the others, I really enjoyed startling people.

*From this carefully drawn study of a foot (opposite), done when he was fifteen, to this still life:* Bread and Fruit Dish on a Table *(above), and then this brightly painted Indian (right), Picasso's progress seemed to go in the opposite direction from what you would expect: his work became sketchier, less realistic, more expressive—and sometimes more violent.*

At the same time I was visiting all the museums, looking long and hard at pictures by painters from all periods, at ancient statues, and at the African masks that people were beginning to collect in Paris. Thanks to these studious hours in the museums, I learned that there were other ways to say things than those I had been taught. One could draw things in another, different "language."

I did not have to draw an eye, for example, with all the details of the eyelashes, the socket, the iris, etc., but two little holes, or just two wooden plugs, were enough to suggest two eyes. The point was no longer to make pretty pictures, but pictures that surprised people, that woke them up to a new way of seeing. I didn't care any more about making my pictures lifelike; I just wanted them to work on the canvas. No more nice paintings for me, only powerful paintings!

*Looking at the* Grebo Mask *from West Africa (right)—in which the main features, like the mouth and eyes, are greatly exaggerated and sometimes extremely simplified—gave Picasso the idea for sculptures such as the* Guitar *(left).*

Little by little, I began to understand that painting was like a sort of construction game, in which forms and colors are combined on a surface. Once I realized that this was so, I began to paint pictures in a new style, along with my friend the painter Georges Braque. Both of us decided to "construct" the images in our paintings using what looked like small painted "cubes," which we put together one at a time, like the pieces of a puzzle, until the entire picture was finished.

For example, look at my portrait on the opposite page of Daniel-Henry Kahnweiler, the art dealer who sold my paintings during those years. It looks almost as if his head and body had been taken apart into little pieces, and then put back together like a piece of furniture, with triangles, cubes, and rectangles fitting into each other. Yet if you look hard enough you can begin to make out, here and there, an eye, some locks of hair, a mustache, two hands crossed one on top of the other, a table, and a glass. Look again—can you see how much the painted face, though seen as a collection of geometric shapes, still looks like Mr. Kahnweiler?

*Here is a photograph of Daniel-Henry Kahnweiler. Compare it with the Cubist portrait (opposite) that Picasso painted in 1910. No doubt you can easily make out the lock of wavy hair on the forehead, the crossed hands, and a small table holding some glasses and bottles. What else can you see?*

In taking apart objects and figures in this way, like when you want to look at the insides of a toy or a clock, we thought we could show all the different sides at the same time: front, back, sides, top and bottom. But after a while, because you could no longer make out what our paintings were about, my friend Braque and I changed our way of working. Instead of creating complicated images by painting many little overlapping cubes, we simplified things and decided we could paint faster.

We started to cut out pieces of newspaper or wallpaper and paste them on our drawings to see what would happen. A piece of newspaper, for example, would be used to represent a bottle, while a piece of imitation-wood wallpaper suggested the body of a guitar or violin. We applied colors here and there to suggest a table or a chair, added a pack of cigarettes, and the result was an amusing new kind of "Cubist" image. These collages, as we called them (from the French word "coller" meaning "to paste"), were like riddles, or rebuses, where you have to put all the pieces together to find out the meaning.

In the beginning people wondered how these cheap constructions could hold together, and what all this disorder was about. Now people seem to understand them better and to enjoy them. Well, the amazing thing is that these makeshift works, which really were put together very fast, often using materials that would normally just be thrown away, are still holding together and are in many museums and private collections today. I used this rather rough and quick way of representing things to make some of my pictures even fifty years later.

Enough talk for now, let's go to the beach. I like to work hard, but I also love to go swimming, or sunbathing, to talk and laugh with my friends, to play with young people like you. I've always preferred the blazing sun and heat of the summer to the fog and cold of the cities up north. Perhaps it is because of my Spanish origins. In fact, when I first arrived in Paris as a young man, I suffered terribly from being poor and unknown. I was cold and hungry like many other people. It made me angry, but I also felt a great sympathy for my fellow sufferers, and I often painted my companions in misery, their lean faces and frail bodies weakened by work.

During this period I used mainly one color, blue—often said to be a cool color—because I wanted to express the sadness, poverty, and solitude of these people. I showed them as silent, still, yet dignified figures dressed in rags, with eyes hollowed by hunger. I drew their hands very long and bony, as if they wanted to hold onto a bit of warmth or tenderness, or a piece of food. For a while I also painted a lot of old men, beggars, unemployed actors, and blind, poor, or sick people, because without any money I had the same difficult life as they did.

*Picasso liked simple, everyday objects; he liked to hold them in his hands, to feel their shapes and the materials from which they were made. In the engraving,* Frugal Repast *(opposite) and the painting* The Blindman's Meal *(above), notice the importance he gave to the bottle and the jug, to the bread and the tablecloth: each thing seems to have its own weight, its particular texture.*

A little later, when things improved and I was less lonely, less deprived, my palette (that is, the colors I used in my paintings) became lighter and warmer. This was known as my "Rose" period, and I often painted circus people, acrobats, and actors. They have a hard and very simple life too, but their laughter, songs, and playfulness brighten and warm the heart.

*During his so-called Rose Period, Picasso took a great interest in the circus and the life of the "saltimbanques" (traveling performers). He especially liked to make paintings of children, acrobats, and jugglers, nude or in their costumes. There was always a special tenderness in the way he showed their activities.*

*In Picasso's work there are often striking likenesses between his life and his art: if you look closely at this figure of a* Seated Bather *(opposite) and compare it with the picture of Picasso playing with his son Claude, you may notice all kinds of surprising similarities. Yet eighteen years separate these two scenes.*

Ah, yes! Here we are. See how the sun and sea immediately make people feel free and happy. On the sand, by the water, the people who are usually so stiff and solemn in their city clothes rediscover that they like to run and play. Once they have taken off their clothes, their bodies seem to become more supple, more graceful. You get the feeling that, along with their heavy clothes, they have also shed the weight of their worries and boredom. That's exactly what I wanted to show in some pictures of men and women bathers on the beach. A new lightness suddenly fills their bodies which seem to become large and flowing before the fluid immensity of the sea and sky.

If you watch people closely, whether they are running or resting, you will see that their enjoyment of the freedom and simplicity of their unclothed bodies makes them actually seem to be longer and taller. At other times, the excitement of playing makes them seem to grow round like the ball they are trying to catch. Some critics have said that I was making fun of people by painting them as huge monsters, but it's not true. When I painted these enormous figures, I simply wanted to express with my brushes the joy that fills each of us when we live by the sand dunes and the waves, under the sun's warm rays. I can also represent this happiness in other ways, practically with just one stroke of my pen, when I draw a very long figure—and a single line is enough to suggest the vast size of the sky and sea in the background.

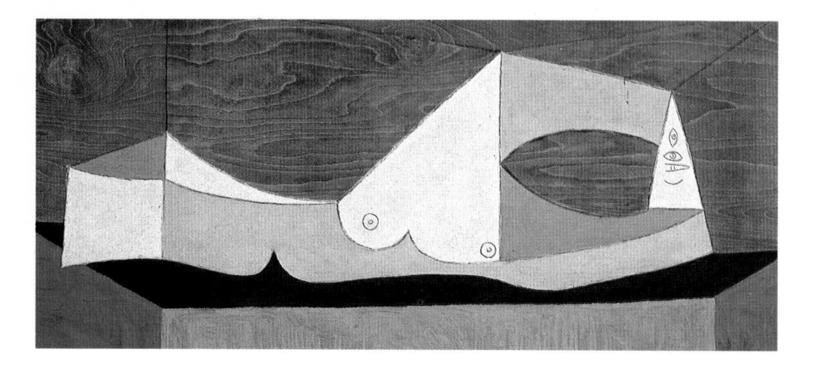

Painters have always liked to paint the human body, especially the nude human body. I have a painter friend who lives not very far from here, in Nice, in the south of France. His name is Henri Matisse and, like me, he's painted many nude figures in his life. Why? For those of us who work with our eyes and our hands, the body is a great mystery that we try to understand. The body of the model in front of us is familiar to us; it is almost like the mirror image of our own body. Yet, it is also mysterious, because this other body does not belong to us—it is under the control of another mind, not ours.

By looking carefully at a body that is not our own, we hope to begin to understand the wonder of life, and by what miracle this intricate architecture of bones, muscles, and flesh holds together, moves, breathes, thinks, sleeps. By drawing each part of the body and then putting them together—the head on the trunk, the trunk on the legs, the hand on the arm, and so on—we sometimes have the feeling we are recreating a living being. Perhaps that is why we are often called creators. In our case it's just an illusion, of course, for the model always gets away; she can decide to put her clothes back on and go off to the movies! But the figures painted in our picture can't leave, they are not alive. And so each day we start all over again to try to find the answer to the riddle of life and to reveal it in our work.

*Picasso often took his inspiration from the painters of the past; he admired them so much that he felt the need to repaint their works in his own manner and not just copy them. He modernized them, like this painting of* The Women of Algiers *after (in other words, inspired by) a painting by Eugène Delacroix, an artist who lived nearly two hundred years ago.*

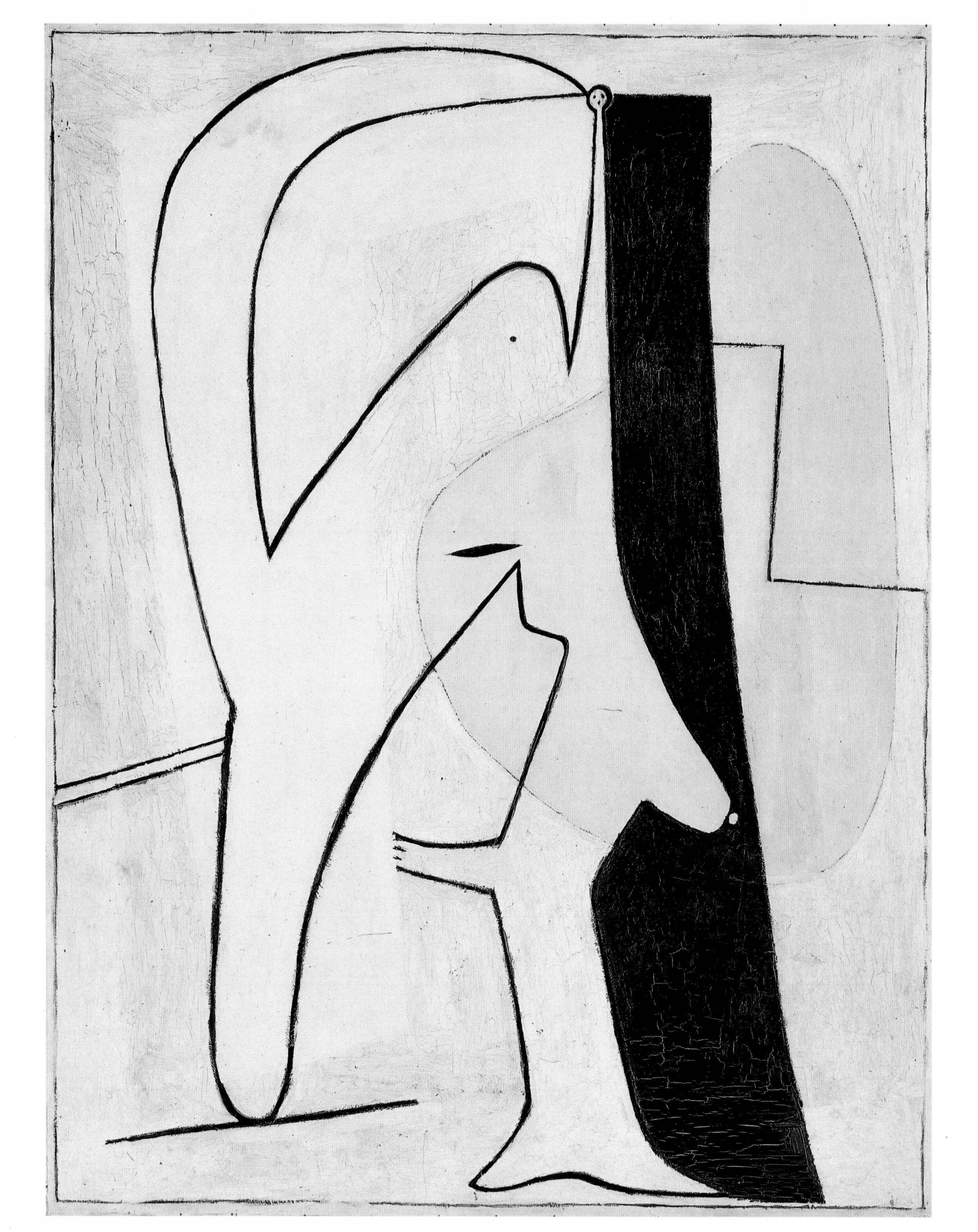

As you know, I don't make a photographic image of a person. I am not a camera! A painter can show a person from several sides at once, picking out what is important and rearranging the parts in a new way into a pleasing composition. But not everyone is pleased by this. As for Matisse, when he drew or painted a woman, his hand moved as if guided by the curves and softness of his models. One gets the feeling that he sat patiently painting them for hours.

But with me, it's just the opposite, I can't sit still. I look at the model from every angle. I'm like a tiger in a cage, and usually I end up distorting the features, changing the proportions, lengthening an arm here, swelling a thigh or a nose as big as a balloon, or diminishing the size of the head until it becomes as small as the head of a pin. I may move the nostrils, the mouth, or the eyes around. A lot of people think that I do it because I don't like women. But that's completely wrong, too!

In fact, it's more like the opposite. Over the years, I have had several close relationships with women, and I loved each one. I painted them over and over again, but since they were all different—their faces and their personalities—and since I knew them at different times, each one reflects a particular part of my life.

*What a contrast there is between Matisse's painting (above), in which the model sits comfortably relaxed, breathing freely and completely at ease among flowers, fruits, and decoratively patterned carpets, and this figure by Picasso (opposite), which seems to have been pulled in every direction, deformed, rearranged. Unlike the work by Matisse, it is not at all relaxed, but tense, disturbing, full of nervous energy.*

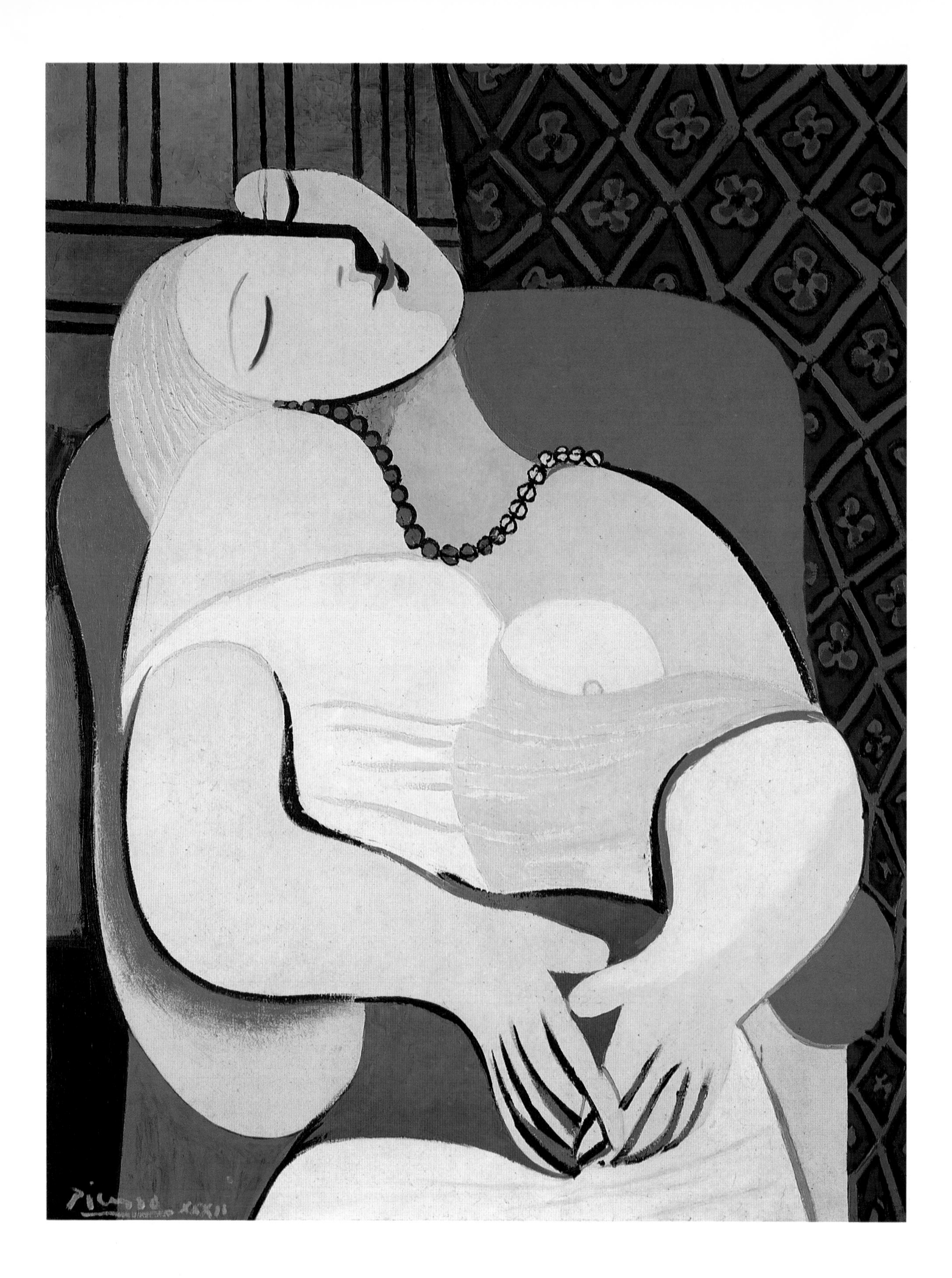

*Here are portraits of three women that Picasso knew during his life: first, there is Marie-Thérèse, sleeping, her contentment expressed in gracefully curved forms; then, the nervous and impulsive Dora Maar, who was known to cry a lot; finally,* Jacqueline, *a portrait of the painter's last wife, Jacqueline Roque, whose serious, somewhat anxious mood is expressed by the gravity of her pose and gaze.*

All of the portraits and nude studies I did of each of them were in fact portraits of the two of us together, our mood at the moment. When I was angry with one of them, or if she was furious with me, then her portrait appears to be very deformed by anger or sadness: the different parts of the face and body are no longer very recognizable and this disorder shows that there were problems between us at the time. But as soon as peace returned, the serene and gentle shapes, and the bright colors appeared once again.

As you've probably learned already with your brothers and sisters, with your friends, and from all the things going on in the world, our lives are in a constant balance between peace and war. Unfortunately, all of us, men and women, men between themselves, women between themselves, people and races against each other, and even animals are constantly fighting and making peace again. Maybe we need this balance in our lives . . .

*This painting called* Cat and Bird *is dated April 1939, a few months before France declared war on Germany and the Second World War began. This ordinary scene of animal life expresses well the anxiety of the painter and all his friends about the rising violence in those days.*

But come with me now, let's have lunch. Later, I am going to take you to see a great, marvelous spectacle—a bullfight (yet another combat!). That's my idea of a perfect way to end an afternoon.

Here we are at last, at the arena or bullring, where we will soon see the spectacle I love the most in the world: the bullfight. I like especially the impressive setting, this magnificent oval of sand, which is sometimes half-covered by a dark shadow, like the sun during an eclipse. From this bright, enclosed ring rise stone tiers, filled with joyful, colorfully dressed crowds, waving their fans and gesturing. Then, above all, the metallic glow of a blue sky slowly shading into night—who could imagine a better stage for this solemn celebration?

The bullfight is a cruel yet magnificent spectacle that comes from ancient times, and we Spaniards perform it better than anyone else. But it is also a dangerous combat; we can't help admiring the bull as much as the man. Here's what happens: from out of one of the gates in the fence below, a splendid black bull will soon rush out, almost blinded at first by the sudden light. It is an unforgettable moment; the proud, wild beast instinctively understands the role it must play as it strides, head high and eyes alert, into battle.

At the beginning, the *toreadors*, or mounted bullfighters, attract the animal with their scarlet capes; they want to observe its reactions and test its courage. Meanwhile, the *picadors* harass and tire the bull by pricking it with their spears. Then comes the spectacular ritual of the *banderillas*: these are wooden sticks decorated with colored paper which a *toreador* sticks into the animal's neck with amazing deftness. After this game of skill, the *torero* approaches the bull on foot with his small red cape, the *muleta*, and begins a long, dangerous "ballet" with him. This is the finest part of the bullfight.

With a series of "passes," which have wonderful names—*veronica, molineta, chicuelina*—the *torero* artfully lures the enormous beast, by then foaming with rage and frustration, to rush past and around his body while he himself does not move from his spot. The bull comes very close to the *torero,* who turns or bends his body gracefully at the very last moment to avoid being hurt by the bull's sharp horns. With each successful pass, the crowd applauds and shouts: *Olé! Olé!*

I admire these *toreros* very much. They fight in the arena, face to face with a ferocious, unpredictable beast that rushes headlong at them with its sharp horns. They risk their lives. At every moment, they face possible death, partly for our enjoyment, but primarily for their pleasure and pride in accomplishing a gesture of supreme elegance. And this is what I find so beautiful and exciting about the sport because this crazy, useless risk is in a way the same risk I take when painting (however, for me it's not so dangerous—I can't get gored or killed—so don't worry!).

Like some of my poet friends, I like to compare the *torero*—that tiny, almost feminine-looking figure in the center of the ring, dressed in his brilliant costume, with his delicate hat and shoes and red cape in hand—to the painter in front of his canvas. If I want to make a good painting, I also have to act fast and handle my brushes with great precision. My subject is there, right in front of me; it even seems to be challenging me. I want to capture it at all costs, but it does not let itself be caught so easily! And then, after I have teased it a bit with the tips of my brushes, which I wave around like *banderillas*, after I have sketched a few lines of the face on the sheet of paper—if it is a portrait—my subject suddenly lunges straight for my eye.

But I mustn't flinch, I have to watch it without moving as it approaches, until it is practically on top of me, almost touching. Then, at the last instant, I step aside and there it is—right in my picture. It is just like capturing it on the canvas, so that it continues its life in the painting. This is why I sometimes say that, like the bullfight, the art of painting is an exhilarating and exhausting game, in which you dare not relax your concentration—those horns are sharp!

*Picasso's extraordinary passion for the bullfight led him to turn out many series of representations of this subject in all mediums—drawings, engravings, ceramics, etc. Opposite, you can see a* Banderillas *scene, a print made from a linocut or linoleum engraving.*

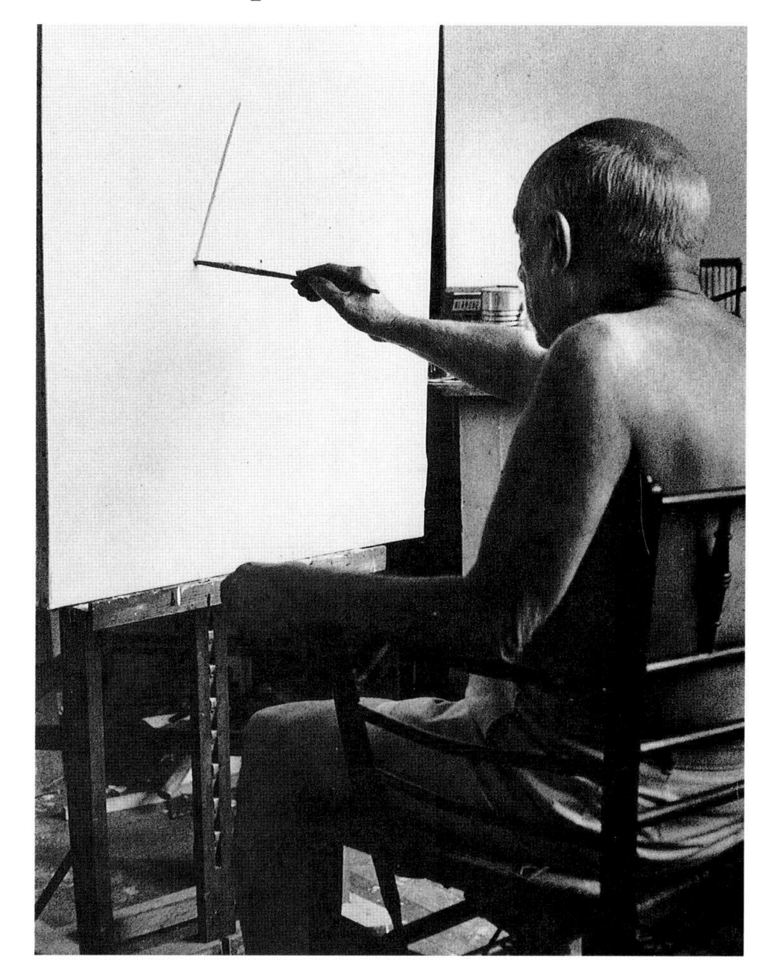

Of course, I don't go only to bullfights. I like all kinds of spectacles. I've done lots of drawings behind the scenes in theaters and around circuses, where you run into all sorts of strange characters and animals, and see many amazing and unexpected sights. I like the feverishly excited atmosphere just before the show goes on, when the actors hurriedly review their parts, ballerinas do their warming-up exercises, and the acrobats rehearse their act one last time before bounding into the ring under the spotlights. I like all these places where people sit in the dark, filled with strange emotions, impatiently waiting for the curtain to rise on a world of color and light, a magical world in which the artist makes us forget for a time who and what and where we are.

*To give an impression of the concentrated effort made by* The Acrobat *as he performs, Picasso represented him in this painting in a strong, flowing arch that describes his body bending completely backward.*

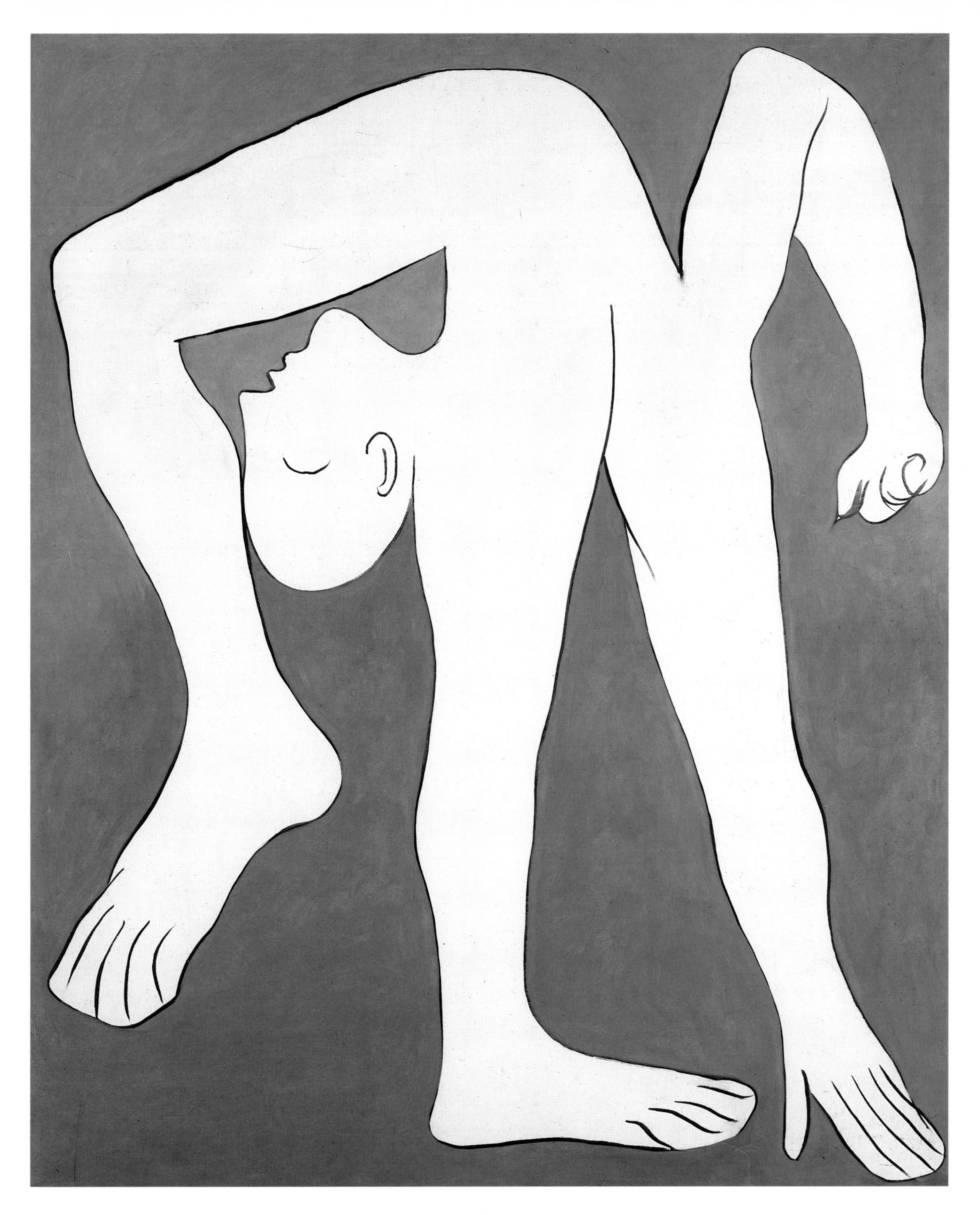

Some things that make us painters dream the most are the costumes worn by actors, the masks behind which the clowns hide their faces. Costumes and masks do not just give us a chance to combine bright colors and extravagant forms, they are also like a second skin, a second face which completely transforms whoever wears them, hypnotizing the people who see them. When you are in disguise or even just wearing a mask, no one recognizes you any more. All of a sudden you are like somebody else.

Maybe you have already experienced this strange feeling? And it's even stranger if the character you've invented doesn't look like anyone in particular, if it's completely zany. In those cases, either you make people laugh or you inspire anxiety and even fear. With my hands I have created so many masks, I have disguised myself so often in my paintings, that some people have said I was like a saltimbanque, a traveling performer casting a spell over people's eyes with my colors. This definition of my craft gives me great pleasure. It is true that I've often tried in a painting to tell a story—usually my own story, hiding it under a veil of dreams and illusions. I think that is what all good actors try to do when they go on the stage.

Picasso
23

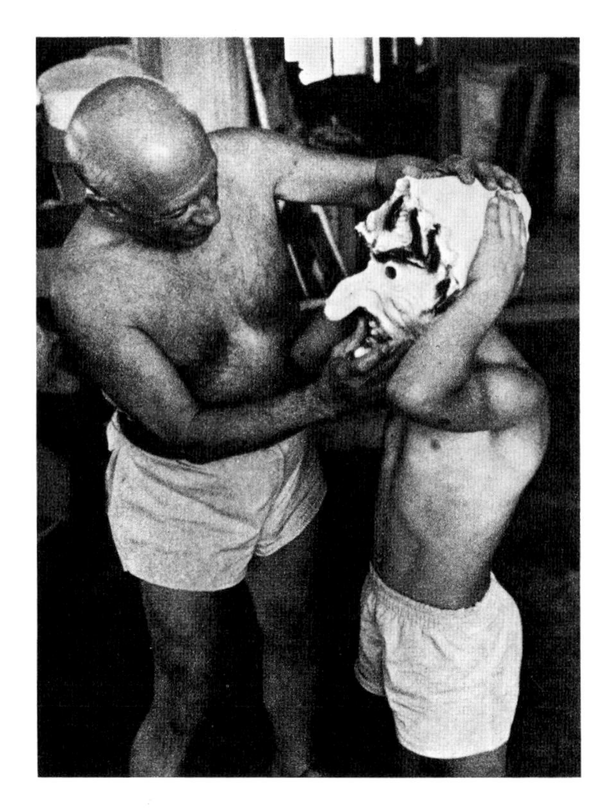

And you, have you ever disguised yourself? What, never? Well, come on then, let's go home quickly. I'm going to make you a magnificent costume. With a piece of cloth, some folded cardboard, a few bits of wood and string, and then a few dabs of paint here and there, I am going to turn you into an African king, a bearded musketeer, a princess, a fantastic animal. I've already got an idea. You are going to look splendid, superb, terrifying!

Come on, hurry up! We have to finish before they call us for dinner . . .

Picasso created
so many works of art throughout
his life that almost every museum in the
world has a piece in its collection. In the last few years,
several museums devoted entirely to his works have opened in
France, the country in which Picasso lived the longest, and Spain,
where he was born.

# WHERE TO SEE PICASSO

## New York, New York
## The Museum of Modern Art

If you wish to spend a colorful day discovering Picasso and his contemporaries, the Museum of Modern Art is a real treat. Because its collection consists entirely of art created during this century or at the end of the last, you will find yourself wandering past one example after another of bright, surprising, silly, funny and frightening, wonderful and weird works characterizing modern art.

Painting, sculpture, drawing, printmaking, watercolor, cinema, even television, all the various kinds of artistic expression that have marked our century figure in this collection. The museum is open—very much open—to new art and a new young public!

Besides displaying more than one Picasso masterpiece, the Museum of Modern Art possesses a great variety of the Spanish artist's works in many of the various techniques he employed and dating from every period of his creative life. You are sure to discover for yourself the many directions in which his imagination led him and may make one or two of Picasso's works your favorites.

*The Guitar* reproduced on page 20, the *Seated Bather* on page 31, and the *Bather with Beach Ball* on page 32 all come from the museum's collection.

## The Metropolitan Museum of Art

*The Blindman's Meal,* shown on page 27, is part of the The Metropolitan Museum of Art's holdings. There you can also see two beautiful portraits, his *Gertrude Stein* and *A Woman in White.*

## Philadelphia, Pennsylvania
## The Philadelphia Museum of Art

As you climb the long flight of stairs leading to the entrance of the Philadelphia Museum of Art, take a close look at the pediments (that is, the triangular spaces just under the roof and so high up on the front of the museum's main building and two wings). Do you notice anything strange? Look again: there on the right, the pediment is filled with statues representing Greek gods and goddesses. Yet the middle and left pediments are empty.

The explanation makes a funny story. Really, artists can be a strange breed—or so some people are quick to say—and are not always the most reliable sorts. The story goes that the sculptor who was asked to decorate the museum's pediments began on the right. The museum directors liked what they saw but, alas, paid the sculptor too much too soon because he left to work elsewhere and never returned to finish what he had started!

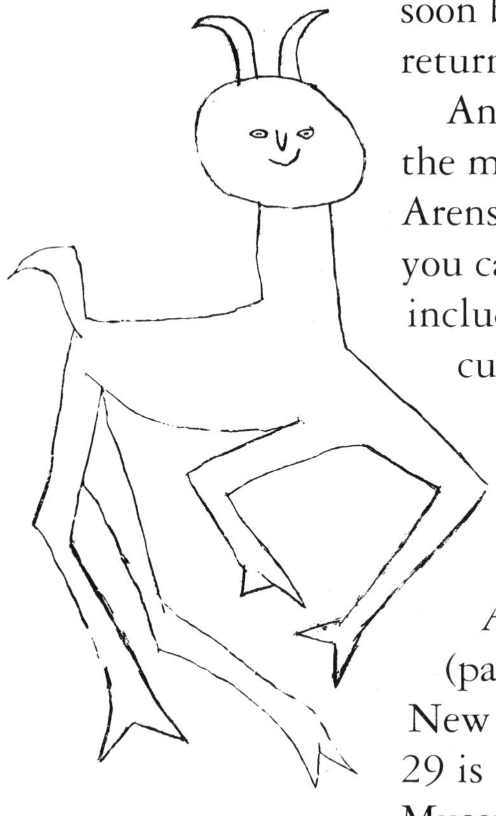

Anyway, that does not take away from the beauty of the museum nor the quality of its collection. In the Arensberg Collection, which is part of the museum, you can find a good number of works by Picasso, including a *Seated Nude Woman* and some excellent cubist pictures, a *Female Nude,* a *Man with Violin,* and another musician, a *Man with Guitar.*

A number of other works reproduced in this book come from museums and collections in the United States. *The Women of Algiers* after Delacroix (page 35) and *The Dream* (page 38) are part of the Victor Ganz Collection in New York. *The Family of Acrobats* reproduced on page 29 is found in the Cone Collection in Baltimore's Museum of Art. And at the Art Institute of Chicago you can admire the portrait of *Daniel-Henry Kahnweiler*, which you have seen on pages 22 and 23. There are many, many more original works by Picasso in museums all over the United States so you will have no problem finding a few like those we have already studied together. Off you go. And good luck!

If you have the chance to visit Europe when you are a bit older, there are no less than three museums that are entirely devoted to Picasso, located in France and Spain.

### Paris, France
### Musée Picasso

The most important of these museums devoted to Picasso was established in Paris in 1985. The museum occupies an old private residence that dates from the seventeenth century and bears an amusing name, the Hôtel Salé, which literally means in French the "Salted Mansion." From top to bottom the Musée Picasso displays pieces representing every period of the artist's life, from the Blue Period to the Cubist constructions to the "monsters" of Surrealism, right up to the last years; even the most classical portraits by Picasso figure in this collection. And above all, you can get to know for yourself the innumerable techniques Picasso practiced: engraving, sculpture, assemblage, pasted paper, pottery, and so on. In the museum's maze of galleries you can have a good time tracking down a number of the works reproduced in this book, in particular the famous *Baboon and Young* or *The Footballer* on the book's cover.

### Antibes, France
### Musée Picasso, Château Grimaldi

If one day you are able to visit the Côte d'Azur (the name refers to the blue of the sky and the sea along this part of the Mediterranean coast of southern France), you should try to stop in the very pretty port of Antibes. It was here, in a magnificent residence situated along the town's ramparts overlooking the sea and transformed into a museum, that Picasso was generously invited in 1946 to live and work in the rooms of the second floor, which were unoccupied at the time. The painter was very happy to set up his studio there and worked long and hard during the five months of his stay. At the end of this period he made a regal donation to the Château Grimaldi's curator, Mr. Romuald Dor de la Souchère, so that the Château was renamed the Musée Picasso.

## Barcelona, Spain
## Museo Picasso

The Spanish museum devoted to Picasso occupies a magnificent palace in Barcelona's old town, where Picasso spent part of his youth with his friends. Most of the works were collected and donated to the museum by Picasso's lifelong friend, Jaime Sabartés. He became the painter's secretary in 1943, arranging his appointments, cataloging his works, protecting him from bothersome visits, and taking care of all the painter's business affairs. The museum possesses a rich collection of works from the early years of Picasso's career as well as paintings from the last period, in particular all the pictures that were inspired by Las Meninas (*The Maids of Honor*), a famous work by the Spanish painter Velásquez.

# IMPORTANT DATES IN THE LIFE OF PICASSO

1881 Birth in Málaga (Andalusia, Spain) of Pablo Ruiz Picasso, who would, beginning at the age of twenty, use only his mother's family name, Picasso, to sign his work.

1891–1901 The young Pablo begins to paint and brilliantly passes all his exams in painting. His first exhibitions take place in Barcelona, Madrid, and Paris.

1904 Picasso settles in Paris, in a tiny apartment (in Montmartre) nicknamed the *Bateau-Lavoir* because of its flimsy construction. The bateaux-lavoirs were well-known washing sheds for clothes, moored along the Seine river in Paris.

1907–1914 After developing a friendship with the French painter Georges Braque, Picasso begins his Cubist period, which will last until 1914.

1917 At the invitation of the Russian choreographer Diaghilev, Picasso travels to Rome to prepare the sets and costumes for the ballet *Parade*, which meets with great success. Several months later he marries the ballerina Olga Koklova. The thirty-six-year-old Picasso is now an elegant young man of the world, moving in fashionable circles.

1918–1924 With his wife Olga and his son Paul, the artist occupies a spacious apartment on the rue de La Boétie in Paris. His work is more classical during these years, his paintings more luminous.

1925–1928 A new art movement appears, namely Surrealism, which brings together poets and artists. Picasso is not a part of this movement, although his style does undergo a certain influence; his pictures become more violent with all kinds of monsters on both canvas and paper.

1929–1932 He meets Marie-Thérèse Walter, a young woman who would inspire numerous portraits as well as large sculptured heads. Picasso sets up his studio in the annexes of the château Boisgeloup, a mansion lying a few miles outside Paris.

1932–1935 Picasso travels, exhibits in several cities, writes and publishes poetry. His friend Jaime Sabartés becomes his secretary. Marie-Thérèse gives birth to a daughter, Maya.

1936 Outbreak of civil war in Spain. Opposed to Fascism, Picasso supports the Republican cause. He is named Director of the Prado Museum in Madrid and becomes intimate with a young painter and photographer, Dora Maar.

1937 He executes the very large canvas *Guernica*, considered to be one of the masterpieces of twentieth-century art, and unveils it at the Universal Exposition in Paris. His new studio is found on the rue des Grands-Augustins in Paris; it is here that Picasso would work and live, alone, throughout the Second World War.

1947 A new woman in the painter's life, Françoise Gilot, gives birth to their son, Claude. The artist discovers ceramics and begins to practice the art with a passion, executing numerous pieces in Vallauris, a small village in the Provence region of France and one of the great centers of fine handmade pottery before the war.

1949 Birth of a daughter, Paloma, second child with Françoise Gilot.

1952 He paints two enormous panels, *War* and *Peace*, subsequently hung in the chapel of Vallauris.

1955–1960 Picasso buys a villa, La Californie, on the Mediterranean coast of France near Cannes. He settles there with Jacqueline Roque, who would become the painter's last wife in 1958. Picasso works diligently on "series" paintings and drawings, free variations inspired by the work of other artists, for instance, *The Women of Algiers* after Delacroix, *Las Meninas* (*The Maids of Honor*) after Velásquez, or the *Déjeuner sur l'herbe* after Manet.

1961 Picasso settles in Mougins, near Cannes. The painter is honored the world over on the occasion of his 80th birthday.

1963 He executes the very important series of works known as the *Painter and His Model.*

1964–1971 Major exhibits of Picasso's work become more frequent. As for the Spanish master himself, Picasso worked almost without pause until his death at 91.

# LIST OF ILLUSTRATIONS

In the following list, the exact titles of the works of art reproduced in this book, the materials used in executing them, and their location are given. A work's dimensions are given in both inches and centimeters, first by height, then width.
Note: the abbreviation RMN: *Réunion des Musées Nationaux.*

**Cover:**
*The Footballer,* 1961. Cut, folded and painted polychrome sheet metal, 23 x 19¾ x 5¾" (58.3 x 47.5 x 14.5 cm.). Musée Picasso, Paris, France (Photo RMN, Paris).

**Page 5**
Picasso as a bullfighter, photographed by David D. Duncan.

**Page 6**
*The Young Artist,* 1972. Oil on canvas, 35¾ x 28⅜" (91 x 72 cm.). Musée Picasso, Paris, France (Photo RMN, Paris).

**Page 7**
*The Artist's Hand,* 1919. Black lead pencil.

**Page 8**
Picasso decorating a piece of ceramic, photographed by David D. Duncan.

**Page 9**
*Girl Playing with a Truck,* 1953. Oil on canvas, 51¼ x 37¾" (130 x 96 cm.). Musée Picasso, Paris, France (Photo RMN, Paris).

**Page 10**
*La Californie Studio,* 1955. Oil on canvas, 35 x 45¾" (89 x 116 cm.). Galerie Daniel Malingue, Paris, France (Photo Claude Gaspari, Paris).

**Page 11**
A child in La Californie studio, photographed by David D. Duncan.

**Page 12**
*Baboon and Young,* 1951. Original plaster statue, small metallic toy cars and plaster, 22 x 13⅜ x 28" (56 x 34 x 71 cm.). Musée Picasso, Paris, France (Photo RMN, Paris).

**Page 13**
*Bull's Head,* 1942. Assemblage (bicycle seat and handlebars), 13¼ x 17⅛ x 7½"

7½" (33.5 x 43.5 x 19 cm.). Musée Picasso, Paris, France (Photo RMN, Paris).

**Page 13**
*The Diver,* 1956. Bronze, 104 x 32⅞ x 32⅞" (264 x 83.5 x 83.5 cm.). Musée Picasso, Paris, France (Photo RMN, Paris).

**Page 14**
*Bull,* 1945–1946. Four states of a lithograph, 11⅜ x 16⅛" (28.9 x 41 cm.). Collection Marina Picasso, Galerie Krugier, Geneva, Switzerland (Photo H. Pattusch, Geneva, and Galerie Krugier).

**Page 15**
*Head of a Woman,* 1954. Cut and painted sheet metal, 34¼ x 10⅞ x 17¾" (87 x 27.5 x 45 cm.). Musée Picasso, Paris, France (Photo RMN, Paris).

**Page 16**
*Head of a Woman,* 1929–1930. Assemblage (painted iron, sheet metal, springs, and colander), 39⅜ x 14½ x 23¼" (100 x 37 x 59 cm.). Musée Picasso, Paris, France (Photo RMN, Paris).

**Page 17**
*Seated Woman,* 1930. Oil on wood, 26 x 19¼" (66 x 49 cm.). Galerie Beyeler, Basel, Switzerland (Photo Gallery).

**Page 18**
*Nude study of a foot,* 1894–1895. Charcoal and lead pencil, 13 x 19½" (33.1 x 49.6 cm.). Museo Picasso, Barcelona, Spain (Photo Museum).

**Page 19**
*Bread and Fruit Dish on a Table,* 1909. Oil on canvas, 64½ x 52⅛" (164 x 132.5 cm.). Kunstmuseum, Basel, Switzerland.

**Page 19**
*Sacrificed Head,* 1907. Oil and sand on panel, 6⅞ x 5½" (17.5 x 14 cm.). Collection Claude Picasso, Paris, France.

**Page 20**
*Guitar,* 1912. Cut sheet metal and wire, 30½ x 13¾ x 7⅝" (77.5 x 35 x 19.3 cm.). Gift of the artist, Museum of Modern Art, New York, New York.

**Page 21**
*Grebo Mask* (West Africa). Painted wood, 14½" (37 cm.) high. Collection Claude Picasso, Paris, France.

**Page 22–23**
*Daniel-Henry Kahnweiler,* 1910. Oil on canvas, 39½ x 28½" (100.5 x 72.6 cm.). Art

Institute of Chicago, Illinois. Page 23: details.

**Page 23**
Daniel-Henry Kahnweiler, 1912, photographed by Picasso.

**Page 24**
*Sheet of Music and Guitar,* 1912–1913. Pinned and pasted sheets of paper 16¾ x 18⅞" (42.5 x 48 cm.). Centre Georges Pompidou, Musée national d'Art moderne, Paris, France (Photo Museum).

**Page 25**
*Bottle of Old Marc, Glass, and Newspaper,* 1913. Charcoal and pasted sheets of paper, 24⅝ x 18½" (62.5 x 47 cm.). Centre Georges Pompidou, Musée national d'Art moderne, Paris, France (Photo Museum).

**Page 26**
*The Frugal Repast,* 1904. Etching, 18¼ x 14⅞" (46.3 x 37.7 cm.). Musée Picasso, Paris, France (Photo RMN, Paris).

**Page 27**
*The Blindman's Meal,* 1903. Oil on canvas, 37½ x 37¼" (95.3 x 94.6 cm.). Metropolitan Museum of Art, New York, New York (Photo Museum).

**Page 28**
*The Two Brothers,* 1906. Gouache on cardboard, 31½ x 21¼" (80 x 54 cm.). Musée Picasso, Paris, France (Photo RMN, Paris).

**Page 29**
*The Family of Acrobats* (Les Bateleurs), 1905. Watercolor heightened with ink, 9½ x 12" (24 x 30.5 cm.). Cone Collection, Museum of Art, Baltimore, Maryland.

**Page 30**
Picasso and his son Claude at the beach, 1948. Photographed by Robert Capa (Photo © Magnum, Paris, France).

**Page 30**
*The Bathers,* 1918. Oil on canvas, 10⅝ x 8⅝" (27 x 22 cm.). Musée Picasso, Paris, France (Photo RMN, Paris).

**Page 31**
*Seated Bather,* 1930. Oil on canvas, 64¼ x 51" (163.2 x 129.5 cm.). Museum of Modern Art, New York, New York.

**Page 32**
*Bather with Beach Ball,* 1932. Oil on canvas, 57⅝ x 45⅛" (146.2 x 114.6 cm.).

Museum of Modern Art, New York, New York.

## Page 32–33
*Bathers,* 1921. Black lead pencil, 9⅛ x 13⅜" (23 x 34 cm.). Private Collection.

## Page 34
*Nude Lying on a Blue Bed,* 1946. Oil and charcoal on panel, 39⅜ x 82⅝" (100 x 210 cm.). Musée Picasso, Antibes, France (Photo Museum).

## Page 34
*In the Studio,* 1953. India ink, 18¼ x 14⅞" (46.3 x 37.7 cm.). Private Collection.

## Page 35
*The Women of Algiers,* after Delacroix, 1955. Oil on canvas, 44⅞ x 57½" (114 x 146 cm.). Victor Ganz Collection, New York, New York.

## Page 36
*Figure,* 1927–1928. Oil on panel, 51¼ x 38¼" (130 x 97 cm.). Musée Picasso, Paris, France (Photo Museum).

## Page 37
Henri Matisse (1869–1954): *Decorative Figure on an Ornamental Background,* 1925–1926. Oil on canvas, 51¼ x 38⅝" (130 x 98 cm.). Centre Georges Pompidou, Musée national d'Art moderne, Paris, France (Photo Museum; © Succession Henri Matisse, 1991).

## Page 38
*The Dream (Woman Sleeping in a Red Armchair),* 1932. Oil on canvas, 51¼ x 38" (130 x 96.5 cm.). Victor Ganz Collection, New York, New York.

## Page 39
*Woman Weeping,* 1937. Oil on canvas, 23⅝ x 19¾" (60 x 50 cm.). Private Collection, Great Britain.

## Page 39
*Jacqueline with Crossed Hands,* 1954. Oil on canvas, 45⅞ x 34⅝" (116.5 x 88 cm.). Musée Picasso, Paris, France (Photo RMN, Paris).

## Page 40
*Cat and Bird,* 1939. Oil on canvas, 31⅞ x 39⅜" (81 x 100 cm.). Musée Picasso, Paris, France (Photo RMN, Paris).

## Page 41
*Bullfight,* 1922. Oil and pencil on wood, 5⅛ x 7½" (13 x 19 cm. ) Musée Picasso, Paris, France (Photo RMN, Paris).

**Page 42**
*Bullfight,* 1900. Pastel and gouache on canvas, 18 x 27" (45.8 x 68.6 cm.). Private Collection (Photo Collection).

**Page 42**
Picasso at the bullfight, photographed by René Burri (Photo ©Magnum, Paris, France).

**Page 43**
*Bullfight,* 1957. Three aquatints, 7⅞ x 11¾" (20 x 30 cm.). Private Collection.

**Page 43**
*A Pass of the Torero's Cape,* 1959. Wash, 15 x 10⅝" (38 x 27 cm.). Musée Picasso, Paris, France.

**Page 44**
*The Banderillas,* 1959. Color engraving on linoleum, 21⅛ x 26⅛" (53.5 x 66.5 cm.). Galerie Louise Leiris, Paris, France (Photo Gallery).

**Page 45**
Picasso with a bull's head mask, photographed by Edward Quinn (Photo © Edward Quinn).

**Page 45**
Picasso tackling a canvas, photographed by David D. Duncan.

**Page 46**
*Study for a Theater Setting* (Pulcinella), 1920. Gouache, India ink, and pencil, 8½ x 10¼" (21.6 x 26 cm.). Musée Picasso, Paris, France (Photo RMN, Paris).

**Page 47**
*Acrobat,* 1930. Oil on canvas, 63⅝ x 51¼" (161.5 x 130 cm.). Musée Picasso, Paris, France (Photo RMN, Paris).

**Page 48**
Picasso with a clown mask, photographed by David D. Duncan.

**Page 49**
*Seated Harlequin* (Portrait of the painter Jacinto Salvado), 1923. Oil on canvas, 51⅛ x 38¼" (130 x 97 cm.). Kunstmuseum, Basel, Switzerland.

**Page 50**
Picasso disguising a child, photographed by David D. Duncan.

**Page 51**
Picasso sporting a mask, photographed by David D. Duncan.

NORTH HAVEN MEMORIAL LIBRARY
3 1216 00179 9159